I.S.A.M. Monographs: Number 10

A Checklist of Four-Shape Shape-Note Tunebooks

RICHARD J. STANISLAW

I.S.A.M. Monographs: Number 10

A Checklist of Four-Shape Shape-Note Tunebooks

RICHARD J. STANISLAW

Institute for Studies in American Music
Department of Music
School of Performing Arts
Brooklyn College
of The City University of New York

Library of Congress Catalog Card No. 78-61291
ISBN 0-914678-10-8

Printed in the United States of America

Published by Institute for Studies in American Music
Department of Music, School of Performing Arts,
Brooklyn College of the City University of New York
Brooklyn, New York 11210

CONTENTS

INTRODUCTION

This checklist is intended to be a guide to the existence and location of a group of tunebooks containing choral music popular in frontier United States during the ante-bellum period.[1] The identifying feature of these tunebooks is their unique "shape-note" notation, which uses four shapes for noteheads, to represent the four syllables of the diatonic major scale (faw, sol, law, faw, sol, law, mi, faw).

Included are four-shape tunebooks published in the United States, 1798-1860; also included are four-shape tunebooks which, although published later than 1860, are directly connected with those published earlier.

The list was prepared using primary sources; advertisements and references to other tunebooks found in the primary sources; library catalogues; and formal lists in secondary sources and bibliographic tools. Where conflicting information was found in two or more of the sources consulted, facsimiles of the title pages were examined or a judgment was made on the basis of the reliability of the sources. National Union Catalog and Library of Congress printed cards were also used as a means of eliminating discrepancies.

Organization

The list is organized in alphabetical order by compiler-author. When their birth and/or death dates are known, these are given with the name entry. When more than one individual was responsible for a book, the names are cross-indexed.

---

[1] Now expanded, this list was first prepared as a working bibliography for the author's dissertation, "Choral Performance Practice in the Four-Shape Literature of American Frontier Singing Schools" (D.M.A. dissertation, University of Illinois, Urbana, 1976).

The title of the tunebook is given as it appears on the title page or, in some instances, as it is catalogued by the holding library. Publication information also represents a compilation of title-page and cataloging material.

There follows information about the size and length of the book. This information gives some basis for comparing the amount of music in each book. For books examined in microform or reduced-size copies, it was not possible to supply dimensions; nearly all, however, are oblong end-bound books about 15 x 25 cm.

Next, known locations of the tunebooks are given. The location list, though not purporting to be complete, is intended to be of assistance to anyone wishing to find a copy of a book. If a facsimile is known to have been published, that information is given. National Union Catalog symbols are used. For private libraries not in that catalog, arbitrarily assigned symbols are given; these are listed below.

The word "urban" is used to indicate that a tunebook contains music that is European in style, "rural" to indicate that it contains music of folk-hymn and indigenous styles.[2]

Annotations are included if judged helpful. First entries give earliest and most complete information. Subsequent entries under the main title entry are listed by date of publication and show only information which differs from the preceding more complete entry. The symbol NI in place of a date indicates that the edition of a specific examplar was not identified by the library holding that exemplar.

Acknowledgments

Roger Fromm, Inter-Library Loan Librarian at Bloomsburg State College, with the cooperation of many other libraries, supplied needed books and film copies. Harry L. Eskew, Church Music Department, New Orleans Baptist Theological Seminary, offered helpful suggestions and provided several fine lists of tunebooks. James G. Smith, now Choral Director at the Eastman School of Music, guided the original research for this project at the University of Illinois. And Rebecca Stanislaw typed, proofread, and checked information for this and earlier studies.

[2]The term "rural music" was used in this sense by William Walker in a preface dated 1866 in *Christian Harmony* (1873), p. [iii].

Symbols for Libraries Not in National Union Catalog

CCMcCutchan—California, Claremont, Robert G. McCutchan
GARHawkins—Georgia, Arnoldsville, James D. Hawkins, Sr.
GATJohn—Georgia, Athens, Robert W. John
GMHamrick—Georgia, Macon, Raymond Hamrick
IPHouser—Illinois, Peoria, M. L. Houser
INIJohnson—Indiana, Indianapolis, Emsley W. Johnson
KYMUWilcox—Kentucky, Murray, Glenn C. Wilcox
LNStorey—Louisiana, New Orleans, Daniel Storey
MIENathan—Michigan, East Lansing, Hans Nathan
NRSmith—New York, Rochester, James G. Smith
NWAJeff—New York, Watertown, Jefferson County Historical Society
OADPovenmire—Ohio, Ada, H. M. Povenmire
OASKettering—Ohio, Ashland, Eunice L. Kettering
OASTopper—Ohio, Ashland, S. T. Topper
OLODFuller—Ohio, Loudonville, Gaillard B. Fuller
OPEddy—Ohio, Perryville, Mary O. Eddy
PBBStanislaw—Pennsylvania, Bloomsburg, Richard J. Stanislaw
THLincoln—Tennessee, Harrogate, Lincoln Memorial University
TNReynolds—Tennessee, Nashville, William J. Reynolds
TXGEOMeyer—Texas, Georgetown, Henry E. Meyer
VIBECarr—Virginia, Bedford, Richard Carr

Abbreviations

c. [date]	=	copyright [date]	imp.	=	improved
ca.	=	circa	inc.	=	incomplete
cm.	=	centimeters	NI	=	not identified
cor.	=	corrected	n.p.	=	no publisher cited
ed.	=	edition, editor	pp.	=	pages
enl.	=	enlarged	rev.	=	revised
fl.	=	flourished	t.p.	=	title page

A CHECKLIST OF FOUR-SHAPE SHAPE-NOTE TUNEBOOKS

1 Adgate, Andrew (d. 1793). **Philadelphia Harmony** or, A Collection of Psalm Tunes, Hymns, and Anthems. 9th ed. Edited by John Jenkins Husband. Philadelphia: M. Carey, 1807.

110 pp.
DLC MWA PHI
Edited version shapes derived by Husband from Little and Smith, as follows:

faw sol law mi

Urban.

2 1811.
Existence mentioned in Lowens, *Music and Musicians,* p. 133.

Aitken, John. See Woodward and Aitken.

3 Armstrong, John. **Pittsburgh Selection of Psalm Tunes** or Ancient Church Music Revived. Containing a Variety of Plain Psalm Tunes, the Most Suitable to be Used in Divine Service. To which is annexed, a few pieces, of a more delicate construction, proper to be performed by a choir of good musicians. Pittsburgh: Cramer, Spere, and Eichbaum, 1816.

111 pp.
DLC PPI
Urban.

Ashmead, Samuel. See *Harmonist.*

Ayres, Daniel. See *Harmonist, Methodist Harmonist.*

4 Ball, Eli. **The Manual of the Sacred Choir:** A Selection of Tunes and Hymns, from the Most Approved Authors, Adapted to Public Worship, to Revivals, to Prayer Meetings, and to Family Worship. Richmond, VA: Harrold & Murray; Philadelphia: Thomas, Cowperthwait & Co., 1849.

15 x 12 cm.
CTY DLC (lost?) KYLOS

5 Bentz, Michael. **Die neue Harmonie**, oder eine neue Sammlung von Kirchen-Musik. Gettysburg: Henry C. Neinstedt, 1827.

DLC MWA PPESCHW PPULC
Rural.

6 Boyd, James M. **The Virginia Sacred Musical Repository**, Being a Complete Collection of Psalm and Hymn Tunes, Original and Carefully Selected from the Most Celebrated Modern Authors, both European and American, and Designed for the Use of Different religious Denominations, Musical Societies and Schools in the United States. Winchester, VA: J. Foster, 1818.

13 x 22 cm. 112 pp.
DLC VIHI
Introduction similar to Davisson, *Kentucky Harmony* (q.v.).
Rural and urban.

Brown, William C. See *Harmonist.*

Brunk, Harry A. See Funk, *Compilation,* 1847.

Cagle, A. Marcus (1884-1968). See *Original Sacred Harp,* 1960.

7 Caldwell, William. **Union Harmony**: or Family Musician, Being a Choice Selection of Tunes, Selected from the Works of the Most Eminent Authors, Ancient and Modern. Together with a Large Number of Original Tunes, Composed and Harmonized by the Author, To Which Is Prefixed a Comprehensive View of the Rudiments of Music, Abridged and Adapted to the Capacity of the Young. Maryville, TN: F. A. Parham, 1837 [c. 1834].

151 pp. 151 tunes.
CLSU CLU IU NCMHI T TKL TU TXFS
"Selected from the unwritten music in general use in the Methodist Church, others from the Baptist and many more from the Presbyterian taste" (p. [3]).
Rural and urban.

8 Carden, Allen D. (b. ca. 1794-1800-d. ?). **The Missouri Harmony**; Or a Choice Collection of Psalm Tunes, Hymns and Anthems, Selected from the Most Eminent Authors, and Well Adapted to All Christian Churches, Singing Schools, and Private Societies; Together with an Introduction to Grounds of Music, The Rudiments of Music and Plain Rules for Beginners. Cincinnati: Morgan, Lodge and Company, 1820.

14 x 24 cm. 199 pp. 185 tunes.
DLC MB MIU-C MOKU MOSHI MOSW THER
Cites "Mr. Wyeth's Repository" (p. 12).
Rural.

9 1825. Morgan, Lodge, and Fisher.
DLC

10 1827. 3d ed. Cincinnati: Drake and Conclin, publishers; Morgan, Fisher and L'Hommediue, printers.
ICU MOHI MOSHI OC RPB

11 1830. 4th ed. Cincinnati: Morgan and Sanxay.
MID MPB OCHP

12 1831.
MOSHI

13 1832. Rev. and imp.: (c. 1831).
CTY OASKettering OCLWHI OCU OLODFuller WHI

14 1833. 7th ed.
CCMcCutchan OC

15 1834. 8th ed.
IN INFWL MOSHI NNHI OADPovenmire OCLWHI PPIPT WHI

16 1835. **The Missouri Harmony**; Or a Choice Collection of Psalm and Hymn Tunes, and Anthems, From Eminent Authors: With an Introduction to the Grounds and Rudiments of Music. To which is added a supplement, containing a number of admired tunes of the various metres, and several choice pieces, selected from some of the most approved collections of sacred music, by an amateur [may be Timothy Flint].

199 pp., supplement 40 pp., 29 tunes in supplement.
DLC ICN IHI MOSW NCD OCLWHI OGRAD OHI RPB
TXFS TXGEOMeyer WHI
Supplement urban.

17 1836. 10th ed.
CLU IPHouser INU KYBGW KYLOS MB MOSHI MOSW NCD
OPEddy ORP THLincoln TXFS

18 1837. 11th ed. Cincinnati: E. Morgan and Son.
CCMcCutcnan CLU DLC KYLXCB MSU NCU NNC OOXM
ORP OU THLincoln TNJ WAU

19 1838. 12th ed.
DLC ICN MIENathan MOSHI MWA N NN

20 1839. 13th ed.
ICN MIU MOHI NCU NNUT OCLWHI PPIPT TXU WHI

21 1840. 14th ed.
MOSHI MWA OHI

22 1841. 15th ed. Cincinnati: E. Morgan and Co.
ICN

23 1842. 16th ed.
ICN

24 1844. 17th ed. Cincinnati: Phillips and Reynolds.
IHI IN INIJohnson MOSW OCLWHI WHI

25 1846. 18th ed.
GMHamrick NRU-MUS OASTopper OHI PPPRHI

26 1848. 19th ed.
IA-HA INU MOSHI
On cover: "Printed and Published by Wm. Phillips & Son. Stereotype edition."
Another edition, ca. 1848, in round notes, by Phillips and Reynolds, Cincinnati.

27 1850. 20th ed. rev., enl. and cor. Edited by Charles Warren. Cincinnati: William Phillips and Co.

200 pp., supplement 68 pp.
CLU DLC GMHamrick ICN ICU MOSHI NCD OFH
Europeanization of harmony and meter.

28 1855. 21st ed. Cincinnati: Moore, Wilstach, Keys and Overend.
ICN

29 1857. 22d ed.
DLC MOSHI ORP PPIPT

30 NI.
VIBECarr (inc.)

31 __________. **United States Harmony**, Containing a Plain and Easy Introduction to the Grounds of Music, And a Choice Selection of Tunes for Church Service, Some of Them Entirely New, Suited to the Various Metres in Watts' Psalms and Hymns, And the Methodist and Baptist Hymn Books. To Which Are Added a Few of the Most Approved Anthems. Nashville: John S. Simpson, 1829.

15 x 25 cm. 175 pp.
CLSU CLU (inc.) IU T TXFS
Introduction same as Carden *et al.*, *Western Harmony.*
Rural and urban.

32 Carden, Allen D., S[amuel] J. Rogers, F. Moore, and J. Green. **The Western Harmony:** Or, The Learner's Task Made Easy: Containing a Plain and Easy Introduction to the Grounds of Music, and a Choice Collection of Tunes for Church Service, Some of Them Entirely New, Suited to the Various Metres in Watts' Hymns & Psalms, & The Methodist & Baptist Hymn Books. To Which Is Added A Few of the Most Approved Anthems. Nashville: Carden, Rogers, 1824.

23 x 13.5 cm. 151 pp.
CLSU CLU KYBGW (autographed by Rogers) T (inc.)
Rural and urban.

33 Carrell [or Carroll], James P. (1787-1854). **Songs of Zion.** Harrisonburg, VA: Ananias Davisson, 1820.

Existence confirmed by William E. Chute in *Musical Million* (1875).

__________. See Clayton.

Chappell, W. L. See Snyder.

34 Clayton, David L. (1801-1854), and James P. Carrell. **The Virginia Harmony**, A New and Choice Selection of Psalm & Hymn Tunes, Anthems & Set Pieces, In Three and Four Parts, Some of Which Have Never Before Been Published—Prepared for the Use of Singing Societies, Teachers of Sacred Music, And Individual Instruction. To Which Is Prefixed an Introduction Explanatory of the System, And a Series of Progressive Lessons. Winchester, VA: Samuel H. Davis, 1831.

167 pp. 191 tunes.
DLC MWA NCD VI VIU
Urban.

35 1836. 2d ed., revised and enlarged by D. L. Clayton. Winchester, VA: Robinson & Hollis.
200 pp.
CLU CTHC DLC IU VI VIU

36 NI.
CLSU

37 Cole, John (1774-1855). **Union Harmony**; Or, Music Made Easy: A New and Pleasing Selection of Psalm and Hymn Tunes . . . Intended for the Use of Such Teachers as Are in the Habit of Using What Are Called the Patent Notes. Baltimore: William and Joseph Neal, 1829.

143 pp.
CTY DLC ICN PPPRHI
Urban.

Coles, George. See *Methodist Harmonist,* 1833.

38 [**A Collection of Hymns,** Printed with "Patent" and "Round" Notes. Ca. 1810.]

NN
First 17 pages missing, including title page and index.
Rural and urban.

Dare, Elkanah Kelsay (1782-1826). See Wyeth, *Wyeth's Repository. Part Second*

39 Davisson, Ananias (1780-1857). **Introduction to Sacred Music** Extracted from the Kentucky Harmony and Chiefly Intended for the Benefit of Young Scholars. Harrisonburg, VA: By the Bublisher [*sic*], 1821.

12.5 x 21.5 cm. 40 pp. 49 tunes.
KYBGW
All three-voice (altos deleted). All but four tunes previously published in Davisson's books with alto.
Rural.

40 ________. **Kentucky Harmony** Or a choice collection of Psalm tunes Hymns and Anthems; in three parts. Taken from the most eminent Authors, and well adapted to Christian Churches; Singing Schools or private Societies. Harrisonburg, VA: By the Author, 1816.

12.5 x 21.5 cm. 140 pp. 143 tunes.
KYBGW MIU-C NBUG NCD FACSIMILE: Irving Lowens, ed. Minneapolis: Augsburg, 1976 [426 S. 5th St., 55415].
Introduction and repertoire copied often.
Rural and urban. Increasingly rural in later editions.

41 1817. 2d ed.
160 pp. 148 tunes.
DLC ICN KYU MWA VIHAREM (inc.) VIU

42 1819. 3d ed.
KYMUWilcox KYU (inc.)

43 1821. 4th ed.
DLC INGO KYBGW MWA NBU TU VI VIHAREM VIHART VIHI

44 1826. 5th ed.
DLC KYU MHI NBUG NCD TXFS VIHART VIHI VIU
Cites "Smith, Little, Wyeth, Billings, Holyoke, Adgate, Atwell, Peck, and many others" (p. 4).
All but two, four-voice.

45 __________. **A Small Collection of Sacred Music,** Chiefly Taken from the Kentucky Harmony and Supplement. Harrisonburg, VA: By the Author, 1825.

12.5 x 21.5 cm. 64 pp. 61 tunes.
ICN
Duplicates content of Davisson, *Supplement.* "Printed by Ananias Davisson, A.K.H. [Author, Kentucky Harmony] for Stephen D. Puller."
Rural.

46 [ca. 1826]. Mount Vernon, VA: By the Author.
ICN NNUT VIHAR VIU

47 __________. **A Supplement to the Kentucky Harmony.** Harrisonburg, VA: Printed and Sold by the Author, 1820.

12.5 x 21.5 cm. 104 pp. 88 tunes.
NNUT TKL VIHAREM
Has little in common with Davisson, *Kentucky Harmony,* 1816 see Davisson, *Small Collection.*
Rural.

48 [ca. 1821-1824].
128 pp. 111 tunes.
VIHAREM VIHART
Same title page as 1820.

49 1826. 3d ed. (c. 1825).
152 pp. 139 tunes.
CLU DNC MHI NCWSM NHI NNUT TKL TU VI VIHAREM

Denson, Paine (d. 1955). See *Original Sacred Harp.*

Denson, Seaborn McDaniel (1854-1936). See White and King, *Sacred Harp,* 1911.

Denson, Thomas J. (1863-1935). See *Original Sacred Harp.*

50 Dingley, Charles. **The Devotional Harmonist:** A Collection of Sacred Music, Comprising A Large Variety of New and Original Tunes, Sentences, Anthems, etc., In Addition to Many of the Most Popular Tunes in Common Use. Presenting a Greater Number of Metres than any Book Heretofore Published. To Which Is Prefixed a Progressive System of Elementary Instruction for Schools and Private Tuition. New York: George Lane and Levi Scott, Joseph Longking, printer, 1849.

16 x 25 cm. 416 pp.
CTHT-W ICN NHD NNUT ODW
Published in both four-shape and round notes.
Urban.

51 1850.
424 pp.
MHI NBUG NNUT

52 1851.
MBU-T PPPRHI

53 1852. T. Carlton and Z. Phillips.
ICN NCU NNUT PPPRHI

54 1853.
NNUT (inc.)

Disoway, G. P. See *Harmonist, Methodist Harmonist.*

55 Doll, Joseph. **Leichter Unterricht In der Vocal Musik,** Enthaltend, die vornehmsten Kirchen-Melodien, Die bey allen Religions-Verfassangen gebräuchlich sind, auf drey Stimmen gesezt: Und mit den vornehmsten Musikalischen Stücken, von versehiedenen Dichtern und Componisten, Sament hinreichendem Unterricht versehen, singesichtet für Singschulen. Harrisburg, PA: Johan [John] Wyeth, 1810.

14.5 x 29 cm. 108 pp.
DLC MIU-C PPESCHW PPLT
Rural and urban.

56 1814.
MWA P PBBStanislaw PLF PPESCHW

57 1821.
Unlocated. Facsimile of title page in Lowens, *Music and Musicians,* p. 133.

58 __________. **Leichter unterricht in der vocal musik,** Enthaltend eine Sammlung Geistreicher Gesange. Vol. II. Harrisburg: Johan [John] Wyeth, 1815.

14.5 x 28 cm. 120 pp.
CTHT-W MH MWA NN P PPPRHI PU RPB
Rural and urban.

Dumas, Edmund. See White and King, *Sacred Harp,* 1869.

59 Ely, Seth. **Sacred Music,** Containing a Great Variety of Psalm and Hymn Tunes Selected Principally from the Most Eminent European Authors, The Greater Part of which were Never Published in the Patent Notes. To which is Prefixed a Musical Grammar, a Musical Dictionary, etc. Cincinnati: Morgan, Lodge and Co., for the Proprietors, 1822.

14 x 23 cm. 320 pp.
DLC F INGO MBU MBU-T MWA OC OCLWHI PPIPT TKL
Urban.

60 Eyer, Heinrich [Henry] C. **Die Union Choral Harmonie,** enthaltend kirchen-melodien, mit deutschen und englischen wörtern versehen. Harrisburg, PA: Francis Wyeth, 1833.

14.5 x 26 cm. 144 pp.
DLC F NBUG OCLWHI PPESCHW TXFS
Bilingual. Revision of Gerhart and Eyer, *Choral-Harmonie* (q.v.).
Rural and urban.

61 1836. **Die Union Choral Harmonie,** enthaltend drei und vierstimmig ausgesetzte Melodien, mit deutschem und englischem Texte; sowohl zum Gebrauche beim öffentlichen Gottesdienste aller christlichen Confessionen, als auch für Singschulen und Privatgesellschaften. 2. und verbesserte Aufl. The Union Choral Harmony, consisting of Sacred Music, with German and English lines to each tune, adapted to the use of Christian Churches of every denomination, comprising a number of the most popular Melodies in the United States; to which is added a number of tunes which have never before been published, some of which have been lately composed for this work, by different authors. Together with a concise introduction to the Art of Singing; for the use of Scholars and persons wishing to qualify themselves

for participating in Divine Worship.

180 pp.
PPESCHW PPL RPB WAU

62 1839. . . . Sechste vermehrte und verbesserte Ausgabe. . . . 6th ed., with additions and improvements. Philadelphia: John Fagan. Printed by J. Vancourt.

192 pp.
NN NNUT PBBStanislaw PST RPB

Eyer, Johann F[rederick]. See Gerhart.

Fleming, Geo[rge]. See Hickok, *Evangelical Musick.*

63 Flint, Timothy A. M. (1780-1840). **The Columbian Harmonist:** In Two Parts. To Which Music Is Prefixed a Dissertation upon the True Taste in Church Music. Cincinnati: Coleman and Phillips, 1816.

22 cm. 204 pp.
CSMH MBHM MH NHI OCHP TXFS
Introduction similar to that of Little and Smith, *Easy Instructor* (q. v.).
Urban.

[__________]. See Carden: *Missouri Harmony,* 1835.

64 Fobes, Azariah. **The Delaware Harmony:** A Collection of Psalm and Hymn Tunes, From the Most Approved Authors: Together with Several Tunes Never Before Published: Containing the Rudiments of Music on a Plain and Concise Plan. Philadelphia: W. M'Culloch, 1809.

13 x 23 cm. 100 pp.
DEHI DEWI ICN INU MWA NN PP PST TXFS
Some bound with Adgate, *Rudiments of Music,* 1803, not a four-shape book.
Urban.

65 1814. 2d ed. with corrections and additions.

112 pp.
DLC MWA PP

Frazee, John. See Nevius.

66 Funk, Joseph (1777-1862). **Die allgemein nützliche Choral-Music**, enthaltend: auserlesene Melodien, welche bey allen Religions-Verfessungen gebräuchliche sind. Auf zwey Stimmen gesetzt. Begleitet, mit einer Vorrede, über die Music, oder Tonkunst; und mit einer, zum Grunde der Vocal-Music vollständigen Einleitung. Eingerichtet zum Gebrauch des öffentlichen Gottesdienstes, Sing-Schulen und Privat-Uebungen. Harrisonburg, VA: Laurentz Wartmann, [A. Davisson, printer?], 1816.

88 pp.
DLC IU INGO VIHAREM VIU
Based on Little and Smith, *Easy Instructor* (q.v.). Mennonite hymnal, *Un partheyisches Gesangbuch,* page numbers.
Rural and urban.

67 __________. **A Compilation of Genuine Church Music**, Comprising a Variety of Metres, All Harmonized for Three Voices; Together with a Copious Elucidation of the Science of Vocal Music. Winchester, VA: J. W. Hollis, 1832.

15.5 x 23 cm. 208 pp.
CSMH DLC INGO MIU-C TXFS VIHAREM VIHART VIU
Thorough introduction.
Rural and urban.

68 1835. 2d ed.

223 pp.
CSMH DLC IEG INGO OCLWHI VI VIHAR VIHAREM VIHART VIU

69 1842. 3d ed., imp. and enl., besides an appendage of 40 pages of choice music. Harrisonburg, VA: Henry T. Wartmann.

15 x 25 cm. 240 pp., supplement 40 pp.
DLC NCWSM VIHAREM VIU

70 1847. 4th ed., imp. and enl. with the appendage blended with the body of the work. Mountain Valley [now: Singers Glen], VA: J. Funk, S. Funk.

15 x 24 cm. 288 pp.
INGO VI VIHAREM VIU
Revised (5th) edition called *Harmonia sacra* in round notes, published at Harrisonburg, VA, by the compilers in 1851. 22d ed. as *The New Harmonia Sacra, A Compilation of Genuine Church Music.* Harrisonburg, VA: Harry A. Brunk, 1959.

__________. See Lewis, *Beauties of Harmony,* 1816.

71 Gerhart, Isaac and Eyer, Johann F[rederick]. **Choral-Harmonie.** Enthaltend Kirchen-Melodien, die bey allen Religions-Verfassungen gebräuchlich, auf vier Stimmen gesezt, und mit einigen musikalischen stücken, nebst hinreichendem unterricht versehen, eingerichtet zur uebung der jugend und zum Gebrauch des öffentlichen Gottes-Dienstes, welches ohne und mit der Orgel kann gebraucht werden, wann ein organist die regeln der Musik beobachtet. Harrisburg, PA: John Wyeth, 1818.

15 x 27 cm. 103 pp.
DLC IU MWA ODW PNORTHI PPESCHW PPPRHI PU RPB
Rural and urban.

72 1822. 2d ed.
GMHamrick MWA

__________. See Eyer, Heinrich G.

73 Gillet, Wheeler. **The Maryland Selection of Sacred Music,** From the Best Authors, Ancient and Modern, In Three and Four Parts. Baltimore: Wheeler Gillet and Co., 1809.

15 x 24 cm. 86 pp.
DLC ICN MDHI MWA NN PHI PP PPI PPL RPB
Rural and urban.

74 __________. **The Virginia Sacred Minstrel,** Containing a Collection of Psalm and Hymn Tunes; Suited to Many of the Metres Now in Use Among the Different Religious Denominations in the United States; and Selected from Celebrated and Approved Authors—European and American, For the Purpose of Public and Family Worship. Winchester, VA: J. Foster, 1817.

14 x 23 cm. 124 pp.
DLC MWA RPB V! VIHAREM VIHI
Introduction similar to that of Little and Smith, *Easy Instructor.* Attacks Davisson on accidentals. Berates taste for "trifling and doleful ditties, patched up from old Love Songs" (p. 4).
Rural and urban.

Goodbon, T. See Jackson, Samuel.

75 Gordon, A. M. S., and T. W. Haynes. **Sweets of Music.** Pittsburgh: Cramer and Spear, 1832.
DLC
Rural.

Green, J. See Carden *et al.*, *Western Harmony*.

76 **The Harmonist:** Being a Collection of Tunes from the Most Approved Authors; Adapted to Every Variety of Metre in the Methodist Hymn-book. And, for Particular Occasions, A Selection of Anthems, Pieces, and Sentences. New Edition, in Patent Notes—Revised and Greatly Enlarged. New York: T. Mason and G. Lane, 1837.

15 x 24 cm. 384 pp.
CLU DLC GMHamrick IAU ICN ICRL MIH MIU-C N NCD NN NNUT OCLWHI OO PBBStanislaw VIU
Probably by Timothy B. Mason and/or William C. Brown. "The rudiments in this work are an abstract of those in the Handel and Haydn collection" (p. [iii]). "The immediate preparation of the sheets, and their supervision while passing through the press, were . . . done by Mr. Wm. C. Brown" (p. iv. Preface signed by Gabriel P. Disoway, Daniel Ayres, William C. Brown, and Samuel Ashmead). *The Harmonist* was a revised continuation of *The Methodist Harmonist* (q.v.).
Mostly urban.

77 1840.
MIU NIC PP

78 1841. New York: G. Lane and P. P. Sandford.
KMK NCU NN OCLLOYD
On cover: 1837.

79 1842.
DLC ICN

80 1843.
Unlocated.

81 1844. New York: G. Lane and C. B. Tippett.
GU

82 1845.
ICN KMK MBU-T VIHAREM VIU

83 [Hastings, Thomas] (1784-1872). **Sacred Songs for Family and Social Worship:** Comprising the Most Approved Spiritual Hymns with Chaste and Popular Tunes. [New York]: American Tract Society, [1842].

19.5 cm. 343 pp.
CLU NNUT PPPRHI

Originally published in round notes (1832).
Urban.

84 [1842].

380 pp.
DLC ICN ICRL IU MB MBU-T MIU MWA NN NNUT ORU PPLT RPB
Different issue from preceding because of number of pages.

85 1842. New York: D. Fanshaw.

DLC FTASU NBUG NNUT RPB

86 1855. New ed. rev. and enl. New York and Boston: American Tract Society.

416 pp.
DLC ICN MB MIU NBUG NNUT NNU-W

87 Hauser [or Houser], William (1812-1880). **Hesperian Harp.** [Philadelphia: For the Author, 1848].

20, 556 pp. 675 tunes.
CLSU (inc.) CLU (inc.) GMHamrick ICN NN TNJ
Hauser was both an ordained minister and medical doctor.
Rural and urban.

88 1852. Philadelphia: T. K. and P. J. Collins.

Preface signed by Hauser in Philadelphia, October 26, 1848. Unlocated; existence confirmed by Mr. T. E. Swann, Route 1, Statesville, NJ, in letter to George Pullen Jackson.

89 Hayden, Amos Sutton (1813-1880). **Introduction to Sacred Music;** Comprising the Necessary Rudiments, with a Choice Collection of Tunes. Pittsburgh, 1835.

Unlocated; existence confirmed by Jackson, *White Spirituals,* p. 25.
Rural and urban.

90 1838. Enl. and imp. Pittsburgh: Johnston and Stockton.

120 pp.
OCLWHI

Haynes, T. W. See Gordon.

91 Hendrickson, George (1811-1895). **The Union Harmony** or A Choice Collection of Psalm

Tunes, Hymns, and Anthems, On a New System of Musical Notation, in Three Parts. Selected From the Most Eminent Authors, and Well Adapted to Christian Churches, Singing Schools, and Private Societies. Mountain Valley [now: Singers Glen], VA: Joseph Funk and Sons, 1848.

117 tunes.
DLC
Later editions seven-shape.
Similar to Davisson, *Kentucky Harmony,* and Walker, *Southern Harmony* (q.v.).
Rural.

92 Hickok, J[ohn] H[oyt] (1792-1841). **The Sacred Harp,** Containing Part First, a Clear Compendium of the Rules and Principles of Vocal Music. Part Second, a Collection of the Most Approved Church Tunes, Arranged for Three or Four Voices; with a Large Number of Select Hymns, and a Few Set Pieces; Designed To Furnish Singing-Schools and Societies, and Worshipping Assemblies, of Every Denomination; with a Complete Set of Tunes, Adapted to All Metres in Common Use. Part Third, a Collection of Popular Airs, and Devotional Hymns, Designed More Immediately for Prayer Meetings and Social Circles, than Schools and Societies. Lewistown, PA: Printed by Shugert and Cummings, 1832.

19 cm. 141 pp.
DLC MBUT MWA NBUG NN NNUT OCLSTM P PPIW RPB TXFS VIU WHI
Recommends seven-syllable round notes as "a high improvement" (p. 4). Synod of Philadelphia: "recommend to the patronage of the churches" (p. [144]). See also Hickok and Fleming, *Evangelical Musick.*
Rural and urban.

93 __________. **The Social Lyrist;** A Collection of Sentimental, Patriotic, and Pious Songs Set to Music, Arr. for One, Two and Three Voices. Harrisburg, PA: W. O. Hickok, 1840.

16 cm. 144 pp.
DLC MH MWA NJP NN RPB
Rural and urban.

94 1843. Harrisburg, PA: Hickok and Cantine.
CTY DLC MH

95 1847. Harrisburg, PA: B. Parke.
DLC

96 Hickok, J[ohn] H[oyt], and Geo[rge] Fleming. **Evangelical Musick**; or, The Sacred Minstrel and Sacred Harp United: Consisting of a Great Variety of Psalm and Hymn Tunes, Set Pieces, Anthems, &c., &c., &c. of the Most Approved Character. Carlisle, PA: G. Fleming, 1834.

14 cm. 254 pp.
CTY MIU NBUG PP RPB
Rural and urban.

97 1834.
MWA

98 1834. Harrisburg, PA: Hickok and Cantine.
15 x 24 cm. 312 pp.
MWA PBBStanislaw PHI PPPRHI VIU

99 1836. Philadelphia: J. Whetham.
MWA PBBStanislaw PPPRHI

100 1837. 7th ed.
P PPLT

101 1839. 10th ed. Philadelphia: J. Whetham; and New York: D. Appleton and Co.
NNUT

102 1839. 11th ed.
MWA

103 1840. 13th ed. Philadelphia: Whetham.
MWA PHI PPPRHI

104 1840. Harrisburg, PA: W. Orville Hickok.
MWA

105 1841. 15th ed. Philadelphia: J. Whetham; and Richmond, Yale and Wyatt.
CTY PPPRHI VI

106 1847. 15th ed. New York: n.p.
MWA

107 1847. Harrisburg, PA: Benjamin Parke.
15 x 23.5 cm. 312 pp.
VIHAREM
On cover: 1848.

108 Hood, George (1807-1882). **The Southern Church Melodist:** A Collection of Sacred Music, Consisting of a Great Variety of the Most Approved Psalm and Hymn Tunes, Anthems, Sentences, Chants, etc. Selected and Original; Intended for the Use of Schools, Choirs, and Social Meetings; Arranged for Four Voices, With a Figured Bass for the Organ or Piano Forte. To which is prefixed, a full and complete inductive elementary treatise, with practical exercises. Philadelphia: Hogan and Thompson, 1846.

192 pp.
DLC ICN PPIPT
Urban.

109 Hunter, William (1811-1877), and Samuel Wakefield. **The Minstrel of Zion:** A Book of Religious Songs, Accompanied with Appropriate Music, Chiefly Original. Philadelphia: Sorin and Ball, 1845.

16 cm. 216 pp.
DLC ICN NNUT PPPRHI
Two-voice (tenor and bass).
Rural and urban.

110 1850. Philadelphia: John Ball.

MWA NNUT

111 1854. Philadelphia: Higgins and Perkinpine.

ICN NN NNUT

112 Husband, John Jenkins (1760-1825). **A Collection of Hymns and Psalms** for the Use of Singing Schools and Musical Societies. Lancaster, 1807.

206 pp.
PHI
Rural and urban.

__________. See Adgate.

113 Hutson, John P. **The Pennsylvania Harmonist,** Containing a Choice Collection of Tunes, Grave and Sprightly, For Divine Service and Musical Refinement . . . To Which Is Prefixed, A Dissertation upon the True Taste in Church Music; Together with a Concise Introduction to the Rules of Music. Prepared for the use of scholars. In two parts. Pittsburgh: Cramer and Spear, 1827.

13.5 x 22 cm. 69 pp.
ICN
Urban.

Ingalls, Jeremiah (1764-1828). See Wyeth, *Wyeth's Repository. Part Second.*

114 Jackson, John B. **The Knoxville Harmony of Music Made Easy**, Which is an Interesting Selection of Hymns and Psalms, Usually Sung in Churches: Selected from the Best Authors in General Use. Also, a Variety of Anthems; to which is added, A Number of Original Tunes; being entirely new, and well adapted for the use of schools, and churches; together with a complete introduction to the proper grounds of vocal music, and rules well explained to beginners. Madisonville, TN: D. & M. Shields, 1838.

200 pp.
CLSU CLU ICN IU
Rural.

115 1840. Pumpkintown, E. Tenn.: D. and M. Shields and Co., and John B. Jackson, Proprietors; Johnson and Edwards, Printers.

14 x 22.5 cm. 260 pp.
TKL

116 Jackson, J[udge] (1883-1958). **The Colored Sacred Harp.** For Singing Class, Singing School, Convention, and General Use in Christian Work and Worship. Ozark, AL: Dale County Musical Institute and Alabama and Florida Union State Conventions, 1934.

16 x 23 cm. 96 pp.
CLU DLC
Based on White and King, *Sacred Harp.*

117 1973. Revised ed. Montgomery, AL: Paragon Press.

118 Jackson, Samuel (1818-1885), and T. Goodbon. **Sacred Harmony**: A Collection of Music, Adapted to the Greatest Variety of Metres Now in Use . . . and, for special occasions, a choice selection of sentences, anthems, motets, and chants, harmonized by Samuel Jackson, with an improved system of elementary instruction. Patent note ed. New York: George Lane and Charles B. Tippett, 1848.

16 x 25 cm. 396 pp.
CTY DLC ICN IEN NN NNUT ODW PPIPT TXFS

Introduction by Goodbon. Another 1848 edition in round notes.
Urban.

James, Joseph Stephen (1849-1931). See White and King, *Sacred Harp*, 1911.

119 Johnson, Alexander. **Johnson's Tennessee Harmony**, Containing I. A copious introduction to the grounds of music. II. The rudiments of music, and plain rules for beginners, exhibited in the form of questions and answers. III. A collection of the most approved Psalm tunes and anthems, selected with care, from the best publications extant; with a few that are original, suited to a variety of metres. Published principally for the use of singing schools. Cincinnati: Morgan, Lodge and Co., 1818.

13.5 x 22 cm. 110 pp.
MIU-C
Introduction similar to that of Little and Smith, *Easy Instructor* (q.v.).
Rural.

120 1821. 2d ed. rev. and enl.

14 x 23 cm. 118 pp.
T

121 Jones, L. J. **Southern Minstrel.** Philadelphia: Grigg, Elliot and Co., 1849.

DLC
Rural and urban.

King, E. J. See White and King.

122 Knight, William C. **The Juvenile Harmony**, Or a Choice Collection of Psalm Tunes, Hymns and Anthems, Selected from the Most Eminent Authors, and Well Adapted to all Christian Churches, Singing Schools . . . Together with the rules of singing, and an explanation of the rules and principles of the ground work of music. Cincinnati: Morgan, Lodge and Fisher

14 x 23 cm. 119, [1] pp.
DLC MWA OC
Rural.

123 1829. 2d ed., enl. and imp. Morgan and Sanxay.

143, [1] pp.
IN INU

124 1831. 5th ed.

130 pp. (inc. ?)
MWA OCHP OCLWHI

125 1833. 15th ed., rev. and cor.
143 pp.
MWA RPB

126 1836. 16th ed., rev. and cor.
ICN OCLLOYD

127 Law, Andrew (1749-1821). **The Art of Playing the Organ and Piano Forte,** or Characters Adapted to the Instruments. Philadelphia: printed by Jane Aitken, [1809].

14 x 23 cm. 8 pp.
CTY ICN MSAE MWA NNU
Urban.

128 __________. **The Art of Singing;** In Three Parts: to wit, I. The Musical Primer, II. The Christian Harmony, III. The Musical Magazine. 4th ed. with additions and improvements. Printed upon a new plan. Cambridge: W. Hilliard, 1803 and later dates.

22 x 13.5 cm. 96 pp.
CTHC CTY DLC ICN MB MH MHI MIU MWA NN NNUT RPB (inc.) TXWB (Parts I and III)
The rudiments were widely copied by later compilers. 4th ed. was first to use four-shape system. Reverse faw and law shapes from Little and Smith's more popular system; no staff, note-locations approximate.
Urban.

129 __________. **Harmonic Companion and Guide to Social Worship:** Being a Choice Selection of Tunes, Adapted to the Various Psalms and Hymns, Used by the Different Societies in the United States; Together with the Principles of Music, and Easy Lessons for Learners. Printed upon the author's new plan. Philadelphia: By the author and David Hogan, From the press of Thomas T. Stiles, 1807.

112 pp.
CTY MIU-C MSAE MWA RPB WAU
Urban.

130 [after 1807]. Printed for the Author by R. & W. Carr.
12.5 x 23 cm. 120 pp.
ICN MB MH NJP NNU-W PHI PPAMP PPPRHI
Other editions seven-shape.

131 __________. **Select Harmony** Containing in a Plain and Concise Manner the Rules of Singing and Easy Lessons for Learners, Together with a Choice Collection of Psalm and Hymn Tunes. Printed Upon the Author's New Plan With Lines and Spaces. Philadelphia: For the Author, by Robert and William Carr, No. 51, Sansom Street, [1811 or 1812].

64 pp.
MIU-C PPPRHI RPB WAU
Re-edition of earlier book with same title; uses Law's shape-note system with lines between notes.

132 Lewis, Freeman (1780-1859). **The Beauties of Harmony**, Containing the Rudiments of Music on a New and Improved Plan; Including, With the Rules of Singing an Explanation of the Rules and Principles of Composition. Together with an Extensive Collection of Sacred Music, Consisting of Plain Tunes, Fuges, Anthems, etc. some of which are entirely new. To the whole is added an appendix, containing explanations of musical terms, characters, etc. original and selected. Pittsburgh: Cramer, Spear, Eichbaum. Printed by Looker and Wallace, 1814 (c. 1813).

13.5 x 22.5 cm. 201 pp.
IA-HA ICN (inc., may be 1816)
Theoretical introduction used by many, including Davisson, Walker, and Carden. Rural and urban.

133 1815. [?]
Unlocated.

134 1816. 2d ed. Robert Ferguson, printer.
MWA VIHAREM (No. 25 of Joseph Funk's private library)

135 1818. 3d ed. Pittsburgh: Cramer and Spear.
ICRL MOSW OCLWHI RPB WHI

136 1820. 4th ed.
MWA NNUT TXFS

137 1828. 5th ed., rev. and enl. Pittsburgh: Johnston and Stockton.
208 pp.
MIU-C NN OCLWHI

138 1831. 6th ed., enl. and much imp. Pittsburgh: Johnston and Stockton.
ICN

139 1835. rev., enl. and much imp. Pittsburgh: Johnston and Stockton.
WAU

140 NI.
IA-HA

141 __________. **Songs of Zion**, Containing a Choice Collection of Psalm and Hymn Tunes, of the Various Metres, used By Christians of Every Denomination. To which is prefixed, a concise introduction to the rules of music. Prepared for the use of schools. In two parts. Part I. Pittsburgh: Eichbaum and Johnston, 1824.

13 x 22 cm. 183, [1] pp.
MWA NN
Rural and urban.

142 Little, William, and William Smith. **The Easy Instructor**, or A New method of teaching Sacred Harmony. Containing the Rudiments of Music on an improved plan, wherein the naming and timing the notes are familiarized to the weakest capacity.—With a choice collection of Psalm Tunes and Anthems from the most celebrated Authors, with a number composed in Europe and America, entirely new; suited to all the metres sung in the different Churches in the United States. Published for the use of singing Societies in general, but more particularly for those who have not the advantage of an Instructor. By William Little & William Smith Copy right secured according to Act of Congress. [Philadelphia, 1801].

14 x 23.5 cm. 106 pp. Lowens edition Aa.[2]
CTHC
Shapes as follows:

fa sol la mi

Daniel Steele may have edited this.
Title page only, 9 x 11 cm., 1798, DLC.
Rural and urban.

143 [1802]. [New York: G. & R. Waite].
Lowens edition Ab.
CTHT-W DLC MWA RPB

---

[2]The various printings have been catalogued in Irving Lowens, *Music and Musicians in Early America* (New York: Norton, 1964), pp. 293-307. Lowens provides more information than is here presented.

144 1803.

108 pp.
Identical to Lowens edition Db except for date.
KMK

145 1805. Albany: Printed by Charles R. and George Webster, and Daniel Steele, Proprietors of the Copy-right.

13.5 x 23 cm. 108 pp. Lowens edition B.
NN

146 1806. Printed by Websters & Skinner, and Daniel Steele.

Lowens edition C.
MWA NCWSM

147 1807.

104 pp. Lowens edition Da.
NCWSM NJR

148 1807.

Lowens edition Db.
DLC (inc.) ICN MIU-C (?) MWA NJR NN WAU

149 1808.

Lowens edition E.
CTHT-W IU MWA NCWSM NNUT NWAJeff

150 [1809]. Containing I. The Rudiments of Music . . . II. A Choice Collection of Psalm Tunes . . .

Lowens edition F.
CTHT-W DLC MIU-C MWA NCWSM NN NNUT

151 [1810].

Lowens edition G.
CTHC DLC (bound with "Christmas Anthem" [n.p.] and Read, *Columbian Harmonist,* 1810) ICN MWA N NCWSM NJR NNUT RPB

152 [1810].

Lowens edition H.
DLC ICN MIU-C NJR NN

153 [1811].

Lowens edition I.
ICN N NCWSM

154 [1812].

112 pp. Lowens edition J.
ICN (?) NN (?) RPB

155 [1813].

Lowens edition K.
DLC ICN OCHP

156 [1813].

Lowens edition L.
MIU-C MWA NCWSM NN

157 [1813].

Similar to Lowens editions L and Ma.
NCU

158 [1814].

Lowens edition Ma.
CBGTU DLC (inc.) ICN MIU-C (?) MNHI MWA NCWSM NN NNUT OCHP RPB

159 [1814].

Lowens edition Mb.
CTHT-W ICN (?) MB (?) MBC N

160 [1815].

Lowens edition Mc.
CTHC MWA

161 [1815].

Lowens edition N.
MIU-C N NCWSM NN NNS RPB

162 [1816].

Lowens edition Oa.
ICN (?) MB N NCWSM NN NNNPSI NNUT

163 [1816].

Lowens edition Ob.
MWA NCWSM

164 [1817].

Lowens edition P.

CTHFW DLC KMK MB MIU MWA NCWSM PPESCHW RPB SCU

165 [1817]. Revised and Enlarged Edition.
127 pp. Lowens edition Q.
CLU DLC MIU-C MDBJ NCWSM

166 [1818].
Lowens edition R.
MHI N NCWSM NHI NN

167 1818.
126 pp. Lowens edition S.
CTY DLC ICN ICU MDBJ MH MHI MWA NCWSM NN OCLWHI

168 [1819].
127 pp. Lowens edition T.
ICN NCWSM

169 1819.
112 pp. Lowens edition U.
OC

170 [1820].
127 pp. Lowens edition V.
ICN ICU IU MIU-C NCWSM

171 1820.
126 pp. Lowens edition W.
CTY MWA N NN OCLLOYD OCLWHI

172 [1822].
127 pp. Lowens edition X.
ICN MWA

173 [1824].
Lowens edition Ya.
MNU MWA

174 [1826].
Lowens edition Yb
CTHT-W NCWSM OCLW OCLWHI

175 1828.

Lowens edition Z.

DLC MWA N NCWSM NNUT

176 [1830].

Lowens edition AA

DLC

177 1831.

135 pp. Lowens edition BB.

MWA N NCWSM VIU

178 NI.

ICN (inc.) MIU-C OCLW RPB VIU (2)

179 M'Cormick, John. **Western Harmonist.** Cincinnati: Looker and Wallace, 1815.

Unlocated; existence confirmed by Crouse and Perrin. Similar to Little and Smith, *Easy Instructor* (q.v.).

Rural.

180 McCurry, John G[ordon] (1821-1886). **The Social Harp,** A Collection of Tunes, Odes, Anthems, and Set Pieces, Selected from Various Authors: Together with Much New Music Never Before Published; Suited to All Metres, and Well Adapted to All Denominations, Singing-Schools, and Private Societies. With a Full Exposition of the Rudiments of Music. And the Art of Musical Composition so Simplified that the Most Unlearned Person Can Comprehend It with the Utmost Facility. Philadelphia: T. K. Collins, Jr., For the Proprietor, 1855.

14 x 22 cm. 254 pp. 222 tunes.

GARHawkins GATJohn NCU TXFS

FACSIMILE: Daniel W. Patterson and John F. Garst, eds. Athens, GA [30602]: University of Georgia Press, 1973. About half of the repertoire is drawn from White and King, *Sacred Harp* (q.v.).

Rural.

181 1859.

CLU

182 1868. Philadelphia: S. C. Collins.

CLU NCU

McGraw, Hugh. See *Original Sacred Harp,* 1966.

M'Lain, Lazarus B. See Wakefield, *Christian's Harp,* 1837.

Mann, R. F. M. See White and King, *Sacred Harp,* 1869.

Mason, Lowell (1792-1872). See Mason, Timothy B.

183 Mason, Lowell, and Timothy B[attelle] Mason. **The Sacred Harp; or, Eclectic Harmony:** A Collection of Church Music Consisting of a Great Variety of Psalm and Hymn Tunes, Anthems, Sacred Songs and Chants, Original and Selected: Including Many New and Beautiful Subjects from the Most Eminent Composers, Harmonized and Arranged Expressly for This Work. Cincinnati: Truman and Smith, 1834.

15 x 20 cm. 232 pp. 128 tunes.
ICN NNUT
"Printed in patent notes contrary to the wishes of the authors" (p. iv), continued after 1837 when round-note edition, *Sacred Harp: or, Beauties of Church Music . . . A New Collection,* was published.
Urban.

184 1835. New ed. revised and corrected.
CLU KU MIDW MWA NCU NNUT OCLWHI RPB

185 1836. Cincinnati: Robinson Pratt and Co.
MWA

186 1836. Cincinnati: Truman and Smith.
CTY

187 1840.
ICN OC

188 1841.
TNJ-R

189 1847. Enlarged, revised and Improved edition. Cincinnati: William T. Truman.
238 pp.
CLSU WAU

190 NI.
DLC F IEN MHI

Mason, Timothy B. See *Harmonist;* Mason and Mason, *Sacred Harp.*

191 Mason, Timothy B. [and Lowell Mason]. **Ohio Sacred Harp.** Cincinnati: Truman and Smith, 1834.

Unlocated; existence confirmed by Perrin (pp. 199, 212).
Urban.

Meignen, Leopold (fl. ca. 1825-1865). See Winebrenner.

192 Metcalfe, Samuel Lytler (1798-1856). **The Kentucky Harmonist,** Being a Choice Selection of Sacred Music, From the Most Eminent and Approved Authors in that Science, For the Use of Christian Churches of Every Denomination, Singing Schools, and Private Societies: Together with an Explanation of the Rules and Principles of Composition, and Rules for Learners. Cincinnati: Morgan, Lodge and Co., 1818 (c. 1817).

14 x 22.5 cm. 126 pp.
MEWC
Rural.

193 1820. 2d ed.
130 pp. (inc.)
MOK MWA

194 1826. 4th ed. By Samuel L. Metcalfe, M. D.
ICN OCLWHI OFH

195 **The Methodist Harmonist,** Containing a Great Variety of Tunes Collected from the Best Authors, Adapted to All the Various Metres in the Methodist Hymn-Book, and Designed for the Use of the Methodist Episcopal Church in the United States. To which is added a choice selection of anthems and pieces for particular occasions. New York: N. Bangs and T. Mason, 1822.

15 x 23 cm. 247 pp.
CTY N RPB VI (inc.)
Work compiled and Preface signed by John M. Smith, Daniel Ayres, John D. Myers, and G. P. Disoway; Committee, reporting in 1821, appointed by the publishing agents of the Methodist Episcopal Church. Later published as *The Harmonist* (q.v). Slight word-changes in title of later editions. Numbers, not consecutive, correspond with those in *A Collection of Hymns for the Use of the Methodist Episcopal Church.*

Urban.

196 1823.

CTY

197 1825. New York: N. Bangs and J. Emory.

NNUT

198 1827.

ICN

199 1829. New York: J. Emory and B. Waugh.

TXFS

200 1831.

CBPAC CTY ICRL NCD NN RPB VIU

201 1833. New York: B. Waugh and T. Mason. J. Collord, printer.

362 pp.

ICN ICRL ICU MB MIALBC MWA NCD NNUT NRCR OCLW TKL VI

Revised from 1822 by George Coles and others.

202 NI.

DLC F

Moore, F. See Carden *et al., Western Harmony.*

203 Moore, William. **Columbian Harmony**; or, A Choice Collection of Psalm Tunes, Hymns, and Anthems, in Three Parts; The First Containing All the Plain and Easy Tunes Commonly Used in Time of Divine Service; The Second, The More Elegant Pieces Suitable for Singing Societies; And Lastly the Anthems; Selected from the Most Eminent Authors in America. Cincinnati: Morgan, Lodge and Fisher, 1825.

198 pp.

CLSU CLU IU TXFS

Rural.

204 Musselmann, S. M. **Die neue choral Harmonie,** enthaltend die vornehmsten Kirchen Melodien, eingerichtet zum Gebrauche aller christlichen Religionen von jeden Benennungen, und auf drei Stimmen gesetzt. Absonderlich eingerichtet zum öffentlichen Gottesdienste, als: Kirchen, Versammlungen und Singschulen. Kom-

ponirt und zusammengetragen von S. M. Musselmann. Harrisburg: Hickok and Cantine, 1844.

14.5 x 23 cm. 160 pp.
DLC INGO NBUG NN PNORTHI PPESCHW PST VIHAREM
Rural and urban.

205 1853.
Unlocated.

Myers, John D. See *Methodist Harmonist.*

206 Nevius, John W. (1774-1854), Cornelius Van Deventer, and John Frazee. **The New-Brunswick Collection of Sacred Music:** Being A Choice Selection of Tunes, for the Use of Churches, from the Most Celebrated Authors, in Europe and America. New Brunswick, [NJ] : J. W. Nevius & W. Myer; W. Myer, printer, 1817.

14 x 23 cm. 72 pp.
ICN MWA NJR PP PPPRHI
Editions 1-3 edited by Nevius, Van Deventer, and Frazee, "Teachers of Sacred Music, in the State of New Jersey" (t.p.). Editions 4-8 edited by Van Deventer alone.
Rural and urban.

207 1818. 2d ed., rev. New Brunswick, NJ: W. Myer
DLC MWA NJNBS NJR

208 1822. **The New-Brunswick Collection of Sacred Music,** Being a Selection of Tunes from the Most Approved Authors. Designed for the Use of Churches and Singing Societies. New York: R. & W. A. Bartow; William Myer, printer.
120 pp.
DLC ICN NJR PPPRHI

209 1827. **The New-Brunswick Collection of Sacred Music:** Being a Selection of Tunes from the Most Approved Authors in Europe and America. Designed Principally for the Use of Churches. 4th ed., enl. & imp. New Brunswick, NJ: Terhune & Letson.
128 pp.
NN NJMO NJP NJR TU TXFS
Increasingly urban each edition.

210 1829. 5th ed., enl. and imp.

136 pp.
CTY NJR

211 1832. 6th ed.
144 pp.
NJR NNUT

212 1835. 7th ed.
160 pp.
CTY NJR

213 1838. 8th ed.
186 pp.
DLC

214 1840. 8th ed.
16 x 25 cm.
NN NNUT

215 1841. 8th ed.
NNUT

Ogletree, Absalom. See White and King, *Sacred Harp,* 1869.

216 **Original Sacred Harp,** Denson Revision. Cullman, AL: Sacred Harp Pub. Co., 1936.
18.5 x 25.5 cm. 461 pp.
CLSU IU LU NBUG NN RPB VIU
Paine Denson completed revision begun by his father, Thomas J. Denson. Based on "James Edition" of White and King, *Sacred Harp,* 1911 (q.v.), with deletions and additions. Increasingly European harmony in each edition.

217 1960. Supplement by A. Marcus Cagle.

218 1966. Hugh McGraw, Chairman of revision.

219 1971. [Sacred Harp Publishing Co., Inc., Cullman, AL 35055].

220 Palmer, James W. **The Western Harmonic Companion:** Containing Most of the Tunes used in Divine Worship in the Western Country, Selected from Eminent Composers. Cincinnati: Morgan, Lodge and Fisher, 1832.
CLSU INU

Shoemaker no. 25657 reports an unlocated edition of 1826.
Rural and urban.

221 1833. 2d ed. enlarged. Louisville, KY: J. W. Palmer and Morton & Smith.

104 pp.
INU NP

Patrick, Marion. See White and King, *Sacred Harp,* 1869.

222 Patterson, Robert (1773-1854). **Patterson's Church Music**, Containing the Plain Tunes Used in Divine Worship by the Churches of the Western Country. Cincinnati: Browne and Looker, 1813.

13.5 x 22 cm. 53 pp.
CTY MWA
Rural.

223 1815. 2d ed. Cincinnati: Looker and Wallace.

CTY OCHP OCLWHI OU

224 **Pennsylvänische Sammlung von Kirchen-Musik**, enthaltend eine gute auswahl von Psalmen, und geistlichen Liedern, u.s.w., mit englischem und deutschem Texte. Zum gebrauche für familien, sing-schulen und musikalischen gesellschaften. Harrisburg, PA: F. [J.] Wyeth, 1840.

ICN
Rural and urban.

225 1844.
160 pp.
ICN MWA NBUG

Puller, Stephen D. See Davisson, *Small Collection.*

226 Rhinehart, William R. **The American Church Harp**; Containing a Choice Selection of Hymns and Tunes, Comprising a Variety of Metres Well Adapted to All Christian Churches, Singing Schools, and Private Families. Germantown, O[hio]: W. R. Rhinehart, 1848.

19 cm. 132 pp.
NCD NJPT RPB VI
Rural and urban.

227 1850. Cincinnati: J. A. Janus for H. S. & J. Applegate.

Unlocated; existence confirmed by Bean (p. 242) and Hamm (p. 308).

228 1856. Dayton, O[hio], (c. 1850).

158 pp.
GEU NNUT OC ODW TXU

229 ________. **American or Union Harmonist;** Or a Choice Collection of Psalm Tunes, Hymns and Anthems, Selected from the Most Approved Authors, and Well Adapted To All Christian Churches, Singing Schools and Private Families. Chambersburg, PA: Printed by Henry Ruby, 1831.

146 pp.
DLC MWA TKL
Rural and urban.

Rogers, S[amuel] J. See Carden *et al., Western Harmony.*

230 Rothbaust, Johannes. **Die Franklin harmonie,** und leichter Unterricht in der Vokal-Musik. Enthaltend, die vornehmsten Deutsch und Englischen Kirchen-Melodien; die bey allen Religions-Verfassungen gebräuchlich, auf drey und vier Stimmen gesetzt: und mit den neuesten und vornehmsten musikalischen Stücken, von verschiedenen Dichtern und Componisten, sammt hinreichendem Unterricht versehen, eingerichtet für Singschulen. The Franklin Harmony and Easy Instructor in Vocal Music; Selected from the Most Eminent and Approved Authors in that Science, For the Use of Christian Churches of Every Denomination, Singing schools and Private societies. Harrisburg, PA: J. Wyeth, 1821.

144 pp.
CTW F MIU-C MWA NN P PHAR PHI PPPRHI
Rural and urban.

231 [1830]. 2d imp. ed. Chambersburg, PA: Henry Ruby.

195 pp.
ICN MWA P PP

Sacred Songs for Family and Social Worship. See [Hastings].

232 St. John, Stephen. **The American Harmonist,** Containing Easy and Concise Rules of Music, Together with a Collection of the Most Approved Psalm and Hymn Tunes;

Together with odes, anthems and set pieces. Harrisburg, PA: William Greer, 1822 (c. 1821).

14 x 24 cm. 136 pp.
ICN MBU-T P PPIW RPB VI (inc.) VIHAREM
Urban.

233 Smith, Henry. **The Church Harmony.** Containing a Selection of Approved Psalm and Hymn Tunes, Adapted to the Divine Worship of the Various Religious Denominations. Chambersburg, PA: Henry Ruby, 1831.

10.5 x 16 cm. 136, [2] pp.
CSMH MWA PPL RPB TXFS

234 1834. **The Church Harmony.** Containing a Selection of Approved Psalm and Hymn Tunes, with Additions and Improvements, Adapted to the Divine Worship of the Various Religious Denominations, and a Concise Introduction to Music; Including Also a Second Part or Supplement, Containing a Variety of Tunes Suitable for Singing Schools and Private Societies. 4th ed., imp. and enl.

11 x 18 cm. 152, 79, [1] pp.
MH-AH MWA NN

235 1837. 8th ed.

296 pp.
VIHAREM

236 1841. 20th ed.

304, 64 pp.
ICN (inc.) NNUT

237 NI. (editions continued to 1847)
CTHC DLC F MWA VIHAMS (?)

238 [Smith] Schmidt, H. **Anhang, zur Kirchen-Harmonie**; Supplement to the Church Harmony. Chambersburg, PA, [after 1831].

Unlocated.

Smith, John M. See *Methodist Harmonist.*

239 Smith, William. **The Easy Instructor** or a New Method of Teaching Sacred Harmony.

Part II. Containing the Rudiments of Music on an Improved Plan. With a Choice Collection of Psalm Tunes, a Number of Which Are Entirely New. [Hopewell, NJ]: William Smith and Co., 1803.

13 x 22 cm. 64 pp.
DLC (no t.p.) NBU
Repertoire different from Little and Smith, *Easy Instructor* (q.v.).
Rural.

240 [1806].

13.5 x 22.5 cm. 72 pp. Preface, 1803.
DLC MIU-C MWA

__________. See Little and Smith.

241 Snyder, William B., and W. L. Chappell. **The Western Lyre**; A New Selection of Sacred Music, From the Best Authors, Including a Number of New and Original Tunes, With a Concise Introduction to the Art of Singing. Cincinnati: J. W. Wood, 1831.

184 pp.
CTY DLC MWA NHI NNUT OCLWHI TMARYC TXD-W

242 [After 1831] J. A. James for W. L. Chappell.

184 pp.
CST CTY CU LU RPB WAU
Rural and urban.

Steele, Daniel (1772-1828). See Little and Smith.

243 Steffey, John W. (ca. 1802-after 1875). **The Valley Harmonist**, Containing a Collection of Tunes from the Most Approved Authors, Adapted to a Variety of Metres. Also —A Selection of Set Pieces and Anthems. Winchester, VA: Robinson and Hollis, 1836.

10.5 x 18 cm. 8, 167 pp.
145 tunes.
ICN VIU
Simplicity was an editorial goal.
Rural.

244 1845. 2d ed., rev., enl. and imp. Harrisonburg: Henry T. Wartman, Printer.

11 x 16.5 cm. 40, 336 pp.
ICN NCWSM RPB VI VIHAREM VIHAR VIHI VIU
More urban than 1st edition.

Van Deventer, Cornelius. See Nevius.

245 Wakefield, Samuel (1799-1895). **The Christian's Harp,** Containing a Choice Selection of Psalm and Hymn Tunes, Suited to the Various Metres Now in Use Among the Different Religious Denominations in the United States: Designed for the Use of Public and Family Worship. Pittsburgh: Johnston and Stockton, 1832.

11 x 17 cm. 160, 40 pp.
DLC MWA TXFS
Rural.

246 1837. Corrected, enlarged, and much improved by Lazarus B. M'Lain.
DLC MWA

247 NI.
F GMHamrick PPIPT (?)

248 __________. **Western Harp.** Pittsburgh: Charles H. Kay, 1844.
CTY DLC F MWA OO PPIPT (?)
Urban.

249 1846.
(See Addenda)

__________. See Hunter.

250 Walker, William (1809-1875). **The Southern Harmony,** and Musical Companion: Containing a Choice Collection of Tunes, Hymns, Psalms, Odes, and Anthems; Selected from the Most Eminent Authors in the United States: Together with Nearly One Hundred New Tunes, Which Have Never Before Been Published; Suited to Most of the Metres Contained in Watts's Hymns and Psalms, Mercer's Cluster, Dossey's Choice, Dover Selection, Methodist Hymn Book, and Baptist Harmony; and Well Adapted to Christian Churches of Every Denomination, Singing Schools, and Private Societies: Also, an Easy Introduction to the Grounds of Music, the Rudiments

of Music, and Plain Rules for Beginners. New Haven, CT: Nathan Whiting for the Author, 1835.

16 x 24 cm. 232 pp. 209 tunes.
Introduction similar to that of Carden, *Missouri Harmony* (q.v.); philosophical material from Moore, *Columbian Harmony* (q.v.).
Rural.

251 [1835]. Spartanburg, SC: For the Author.
CLU

252 1845. Philadelphia: Thomas, Cowperthwait & Co.
KYLOS

253 1847. New edition, improved and enlarged. Philadelphia: Cowperthwait.
304 pp.
CLU (inc.) TXFS

254 1847. Philadelphia: E. W. Miller.
NNUT

255 1851. Philadelphia: Cowperthwait.
ICN

256 1854. New edition, thoroughly revised and greatly improved. Philadelphia: E. W. Miller.
336 pp. 295 tunes.
CLU ICN FACSIMILE: New York: Hastings House, 1939.
For Young Men's Progress Club, Benton, KY. Twenty-two pages of introductory material on "The Big Singing." FACSIMILE: Glenn C. Wilcox, ed. Los Angeles: Pro Musicamericana, 1966 [now: 703 Earl Ct., Murray, KY 42071].

257 1854. Philadelphia: Miller and Burlock.
NRSmith TNSB TXFS
Identical to E. W. Miller edition.

258 NI.
DLC GMHamrick VIHAMS (?)

259 __________. **The Southern and Western Pocket Harmonist,** Intended as an Appendix to The Southern Harmony; Embracing the Principal Hymns, Songs, Choruses, and Re-

vival Tunes, Usually Sung at Protracted and Campmeetings of Different Denominations of Christians throughout the Southern and Western States; Also, a Number of Choice Pieces for the Church and Social Singing Societies, To Which Is Prefixed, a Concise Introductory to the Grounds of Music. Philadelphia: Cowperthwait and Co., 1846 (c. 1845).

14 x 22 cm. 175 pp. 126 tunes (inc.)
CLSU CLU CTHC DLC (inc.) IU NNHI RPB
Rural.

Warren, Charles. See Carden, *Missouri Harmony,* 1850.

260 Weber, T[homas] R. **The Juvenile Harmony.** [Allentown, PA], 1852.
Unlocated; mentioned by Eskew.

261 1859.
PBBStanislaw

262 __________. **The Juvenile Singing School.** [Allentown, PA], 1855.
Unlocated; mentioned by Eskew.

263 __________. **The New Harmony** . . . Neue Harmonie [Allentown, PA], 1855.
Unlocated; mentioned by Eskew. May be same as 2d edition of *Die neue Choral Harmonie* (below).

264 __________. **Die neue Choral Harmonie.** Hellertown, PA, 1853.
Unlocated; mentioned by Eskew.

265 1855.
Unlocated. See Weber, *The New Harmony.*

266 __________. **Die Pennsylvänische Choral Harmonie.** The Pennsylvania Choral Harmony, Containing the Principal Church Melodies Provided with German and English Text. Allentown, PA: By the Compiler, 1844.

17 x 27 cm. 292 pp. 340 tunes.
DLC PBBStanislaw (?, no t.p.)
Rural and urban.

267 1849. 2d ed.

268 1859. 5th ed.
DLC

269 1867. Hellertown, PA.

270 1870. 8th ed. Printed by Wm. H. Knauss, Hellertown, PA.

271 NI.

376 pp.
PBBStanislaw (no t.p.)

272 ______. **Pennsylvänische Sammlung von Kirchen-Musick.** [Allentown, PA]: By the Compiler, 1859.

DLC
Not the same as Weber, *Pennsylvania Choral Harmony,* 5th ed.
Rural and urban.

273 White, Benjamin Franklin (1800-1879), and E. J. King. **The Sacred Harp,** a Collection of Psalm and Hymn Tunes, Odes, and Anthems, Selected from the Most Eminent Authors: Together with Nearly One Hundred Pieces Never Before Published; Suited to Most Metres, And Well Adapted to Churches of Every Denomination, Singing Schools, and Private Societies. With plain rules for learners. Philadelphia: B. F. White and Joel [E. J. or a brother] King, 1844.

263 pp.
Introduction almost duplicates Walker, *Southern Harmony* (q.v.). Editions in 1870 and 1911 were co-authored by D. P. White (see White and White); "Cooper editions" appeared in 1902, 1909, 1949, and 1960; *Original Sacred Harp* editions appeared in 1936, 1960, 1966, and 1971.
DLC

274 1847. Philadelphia: T. K. & P. G. Collins.

KYLOS

275 1850. 2d ed. Philadelphia: S. C. Collins, Jr.

22.5 x 14 cm. 262 pp., appendix 104 pp.
TXFS TXWB

276 1859. 3d ed. New and much improved and enlarged edition.

366 pp., appendix 66 pp. 413 tunes.
TXFS
Most complete edition by B. F. White.

277 1860.

CLU TNReynolds TXFS FACSIMILE: William B. Reynolds, ed. Nashville, TN: Broadman Press, 1968 [127 Ninth Ave. N., 37203].

Imprint of 1859 edition.

278 1869. 4th ed. entirely remodeled containing one hundred and thirty new and selected pieces, expressly arranged and prepared for this book, compiled by a committee appointed by "The Southern Musical Convention." Atlanta: Charles P. Byrd.

477 pp.
CLU (inc.) KYLOS (inc.) TXFS
Edited by Edmund Dumas, Absalom Ogletree, R. F. M. Mann, and Marion Patrick. Compare White and White, *Sacred Harp,* 1911.

279 1911. Cullman, AL: Sacred Harp Pub. Co.

550 pp.
"James edition"—Joseph Stephen James, ed. Seaborn McDaniel Denson, musical ed., added alto parts to most (327) of originally three-voice tunes.

280 1929. [5th ed. of J. S. James revision (1911)]. Atlanta: Ruralist Press.

CLU

281 NI.

TXFS

__________. See Jackson, Judge.

__________. See *Original Sacred Harp.*

__________. See White and White.

282 White, Benjamin Franklin, and D[avid] P[atillo] White. **The Sacred Harp** . . . 1870.

Identical to White and King, *Sacred Harp,* 1869 (q.v.), except preface, by B. F. White alone. Not the same as *The New Sacred Harp* by two of White's sons, 1884, a seven-shape tunebook.

283 1902. Rev. and imp. Dothan, AL: W. M. Cooper.

"Cooper edition." "Corrected" and modernized—no longer in the tradition of the 1844 edition.

284 1909. Panama City, FL: Blackshear.

CLU DLC

285 1911.
1870 original plates plus 73 new pages of urban tunes.

"James L. White edition"—chief editor.
TXFS

286 1949. Troy and Dothan, AL: W. M. Cooper.

NCD

287 1960. 12th ed. Troy, AL: Sacred Harp Book Co.

288 Willis, Robert. **Lexington Cabinet and Repository of Sacred Music.** Louisville, KY: Norwood and Palmer, 1832 (1831?).

DLC N
Rural.

289 NI.

LNStorey

290 Winebrenner, John (1797-1860), and Leopold Meignen. **The Seraphina.** Harrisburg, PA: By the Compiler, 1854.

DLC
Theoretical introduction by Meignen. Published in two different versions, one four-shape and one round, "to gratify the tastes and preferences of people in different parts of the country" (p. 2).
Urban.

291 Woodbury, Isaac Baker (1819-1858). **Harp of the South.** New York: Mason Brothers, 1853.

320 pp.
GMHamrick MWA
Published in both four-shape and round notes.
Urban.

292 Woodward, Charles. **Sacred Music in Miniature**; Containing a Choice Selection of Nearly One Hundred and Fifty Psalm and Hymn Tunes, Set in Three Parts.—Chiefly New: Adapted to Public and Family Worship, and Including a Great Variety of Metres from Dr. Watts', Rippon's, the Methodist, and Other Hymn Books: A Great Proportion of Which Are the Production of a Celebrated Composer in England, Where They are Highly Esteemed Together with Others Composed Expressly for the Work. Philadelphia: M. Cary for W. W. Woodward, 1812.

7.5 x 11.5 cm. 208 pp.

CTHC DLC MBHM MWA PPPRHI
Similar to Little and Smith, *Easy Instructor,* later editions (q.v.).
Urban.

293 Woodward, Charles, and John Aitken. **Ecclesiae Harmonia.** A Selection of Sacred Music. Philadelphia: By the Author, 1807.

14.8 x 26 cm. 100 pp.
CTY CYHC DLC MB MHI MWA NJR NRU PHI PPIPT
Variant on shape-note system:

fa sol la mi

Rural and urban.

294 [ca. 1807].

CTHC
Identical to preceding except pp. 7-8 omitted.

295 [1809]. 2d ed. Improved and enlarged by the addition of upwards of 40 tunes including anthems and pieces. Philadelphia: W. W. Woodward.

13.8 x 22.5 cm. 108 pp.
CTHC CTY DLC MB MH MHI MWA NJR PHI

296 Wyeth, John (1770-1858). **Wyeth's Repository of Sacred Music.** Selected from the most eminent and approved authors in that science, For the use of Christian Churches of every denomination, Singing Schools and Private Societies. Together with a plain and concise Introduction to the Grounds of Music, And Rules for learners. Harrisburg, PA: John Wyeth, 1810.

14.5 x 24.5 cm. 120 pp.
MWA OCLWHI P PHAR
Widely copied by the German four-shape book compilers.
Rural and urban.

297 1811. 2d ed.

MWA P PST

298 1812. 3d ed.

132 pp.
ICN MWA

299 1818. 4th ed.

ICN MWA OCLWHI PHI PLF PPESCHW

300 1820. 5th ed.

DLC GMHamrick MBHM NN OCLWHI P PHAR PLF PPIPT

301 1826. [6th ed.] improved and corrected.

144 pp.
IA-HI ICN MH PBBStanislaw PHI

302 1834. Unlocated.

303 ________. **Wyeth's Repository of Sacred Music. Part Second.** Original and Selected from the Most Eminent and Approved Authors in That Science. For the Use of Christian Churches, Singing Schools and Private Societies. Together with a Plain and Concise Introduction to the Grounds of Music, and Rules for Learners. Harrisburg, PA: John Wyeth, 1813.

14.5 x 24.5 cm. 132 pp. 149 tunes.
MWA OCLWHI PLF
Introduction [and musical editing] by E. K. Dare. Rev. Dare's introduction copied by Davisson, Carden, Moore, Rhinehart, and others. A number of tunes concordant with those in Ingall's *Christian Harmony.*

Rural and urban.

304 1820. 2d ed.

DLC ICN LNB MWA NBUG OCLWHI OO PHI PPIPT RPB TXFS TXU FACSIMILE: Irving Lowens, ed. New York: Da Capo, 1964 [227 West 17th Street, NY 10011].

305 **Zion's Harp.** Cincinnati: J. A. James for J. Fisher & Son, 1836.

Unlocated.

BIBLIOGRAPHY OF SECONDARY SOURCES

Arrington, Elwyn Golden. "Nationalism and American Music, 1790-1815." Ph.D. dissertation, The University of Texas at Austin, 1969.

Baer, Elizabeth. "Music: An Integral Part of Life in Ohio 1800-1860." Ohio Historical and Philosophical Society Bulletin 14 (July 1956): 197-210.

Bean, Shirley Ann. "*The Missouri Harmony,* 1820-1858: The Refinement of a Southern Tunebook." D.M.A. dissertation, University of Missouri-Kansas City, 1973.

Bio-Bibliographical Index of Musicians in the United States of America. 2d ed. Washington, D.C.: Historical Records Survey, Music Section, Pan American Union, 1956; reprint ed., New York: Da Capo, 1971.

Britton, Allen P. "Theoretical Introductions in American Tune-Books to 1800." Ph.D. dissertation, University of Michigan, 1949.

Chase, Gilbert. America's Music: From the Pilgrims to the Present. Rev. 2d ed. New York: McGraw-Hill, 1966.

Cheek, Curtis Leo. "The Singing School and Shaped-Note Tradition: Residuals in Twentieth Century Hymnody." D.M.A. dissertation, University of Southern California, 1968.

Crouse, David Lee. "The Work of Allen D. Carden and Associates in the Shape-Note Tune-Books, *The Missouri Harmony, Western Harmony* and *United States Harmony.*" D.M.A. dissertation, Southern Baptist Theological Seminary, 1972.

Ellington, Charles Linwood. "The Sacred Harp Tradition of the South: Its Origin and Evolution." Ph.D. dissertation, Florida State University at Tallahassee, 1969.

Eskew, Harry Lee. "Shape-Note Hymnody in the Shenandoah Valley, 1816-1860." Ph.D. dissertation, Tulane University, 1966.

Evans, Charles. American Bibliography: 1639-1820 A. D. 14 vols. New York: Peter Smith, 1941-1959.

Hall, James W., Jr. "The Tune-Book in American Culture." Ph.D. dissertation, University of Pennsylvania, 1967.

Hamm, Charles. "Patent Notes in Cincinnati." Bulletin, Historical and Philosophical Society of Ohio 16 (October 1958): 293-310.

Harley, Rachel August Brett. "Ananias Davisson: Southern Tune-Book Compiler (1780-1857)." Ph.D. dissertation, University of Michigan, 1972.

Haywood, Charles. A Bibliography of North American Folklore and Folksong. 2 vols. 2d ed. New York: Dover, 1961.

Jackson, George Pullen. Another Sheaf of White Spirituals. Gainesville: University of Florida Press, 1952.

__________. Down-East Spirituals and Others. 2d ed. New York: J. J. Augustin, 1943.

__________. Spiritual Folk Songs of Early America. New York: J. J. Augustin, 1937; reprint ed., New York: Dover, 1964.

__________. The Story of the *Sacred Harp* 1844-1944. Nashville: Vanderbilt University Press, 1944.

__________. White and Negro Spirituals. Locust Valley, NY: J. J. Augustin, 1943.

__________. White Spirituals in the Southern Uplands. Chapel Hill: University of North Carolina Press, 1933.

Jackson, Richard. United States Music: Sources of Bibliography and Collective Biography. Institute for Studies in American Music Monograph No. 1. Brooklyn, NY: Institute for Studies in American Music, 1973.

Krohn, Ernst Christopher. A Century of Missouri Music. St. Louis: By the Author, 1924. Reprinted in *Missouri Music* by E. C. Krohn, pp. xli-134. New York: Da Capo, 1971.

__________. "A Checklist of Editions of *The Missouri Harmony.*" Missouri Historical Society Bulletin 6 (April 1950): 374-399. Reprinted in *Missouri Music* by E. C. Krohn, pp. 199-225. New York: Da Capo, 1971.

__________. "*The Missouri Harmony,* a Study in Early American Psalmody." Missouri Historical Society Bulletin 6 (October 1949): 25-33. Reprinted in *Missouri Music* by E. C. Krohn, pp. 187-197. New York: Da Capo, 1971.

__________. Missouri Music. New York: Da Capo, 1971.

Lindsley, Charles Edward. "Early Nineteenth-Century American Collections of Sacred Choral Music, 1800-1810: Part I, a Historical Survey of Tunebook Production to 1810; Part II, an Annotated Bibliography of Tunebooks, 1800-1810." Ph.D. dissertation, University of Iowa, 1968.

Lowens, Irving. "Introduction" to facsimile edition of *Kentucky Harmony,* by Ananias Davisson, pp. 3-16. Minneapolis: Augsburg, 1976.

__________. "Introduction" to facsimile edition of *Wyeth's Repository of Sacred Music, Part Second,* by John Wyeth, pp. v-vi. New York: Da Capo Press, 1964.

__________. Music and Musicians in Early America. New York: Norton, 1964.

Macdougall, Hamilton C. Early New England Psalmody—An Historical Appreciation 1620-1820. Brattleboro: Stephen Daye, 1940.

McMurtrie, Douglas Crawford. Early Printing in Tennessee, with a Bibliography of the Issues of the Tennessee Press 1973-1830. Chicago: Chicago Club of Printing House Craftsmen, 1933.

Marrocco, Thomas, and Harold Gleason, eds. Music in America, an Anthology from the Landing of the Pilgrims to the Close of the Civil War, 1620-1865. New York: Norton, 1964.

Metcalf, Frank Johnson. American Psalmody; or, Titles of Books, Containing Tunes Printed in America from 1721-1820. New York: C. F. Heartman, 1917.

__________. American Writers and Compilers of Sacred Music. Nashville, Abingdon, 1925.

Mott, Frank Luther. Golden Multitudes; The Story of Best Sellers in the United States. New York: Macmillan, 1947.

The Musical Million [monthly]. Dayton, Rockingham County, VA: Ruebush, Kieffer and Co., 1870-1913.

Original Sacred Harp. Denson Revision. Cullman, AL: Sacred Harp Pub. Co., 1971.

Perrin, Phil D. "Theoretical Introductions in American Tune-Books from 1801-1860." D.M.A. dissertation, Southwest Baptist Theological Seminary, Ft. Worth, 1969.

Revitt, Paul J., comp. The George Pullen Jackson Collection of Southern Hymnody; a Bibliography, with an Introduction. Los Angeles: University of California Library, 1964.

Reynolds, William Jensen. Postscript to the facsimile edition of *Sacred Harp*, by B. F. White and E. J. King, pp. xxi-xxv. Nashville: Broadman, 1968.

Rosewall, Richard B. "Singing Schools in Pennsylvania: 1800-1900." Ph.D. dissertation, University of Minnesota, 1969.

Sabin, Robert. "Early American Composers and Critics." Musical Quarterly 24 (April 1938): 210-218.

Scholten, James William. "The Chapins: A Study of Men and Sacred Music West of the Alleghenies, 1795-1842." Ed.D. dissertation, University of Michigan, 1972.

Shaw, Ralph R., and Richard H. Shoemaker. American Bibliography: A Preliminary Checklist, 1801-1819. New York: Scarecrow Press, 1958-1966.

Shipton, Clifford Kenyon, and James E. Mooney. National Index of American Imprints through 1800; The Short-Title Evans. Worcester, MA: American Antiquarian Society, 1969.

Shoemaker, Richard H. A Checklist of American Imprints for 1820-1830. New York: Scarecrow Press, 1964-1972.

Sims, John Norman. "The Hymnody of the Camp Meeting Tradition." S.M.D. thesis, Union Theological Seminary, 1960.

Stanislaw, Richard J. "Choral Performance Practice in the Four-Shape Literature of American Frontier Singing Schools." D.M.A. dissertation, University of Illinois, 1976.

Stevenson, Robert Murrell. Protestant Church Music in America. New York: Norton, 1966.

Sutton, Walter. The Western Book Trade: Cincinnati as a Nineteenth-Century Publishing and Book-Trade Center. Columbus: Ohio State University Press, 1961.

Sweet, William Warren. Religion on the American Frontier: 1783-1840. 4 vols. Reprint ed., New York: Cooper Square, 1964. Vol. 1: The Baptists. New York: Harper, 1931; Vol. 2: The Presbyterians. New York: Harper, 1936; Vol. 3: The Congregationalists. New York: Harper, 1939; Vol. 4: The Methodists. Chicago: University of Chicago Press, 1946.

__________. Revivalism in America, Its Origin, Growth, and Decline. New York: Scribner, 1945; reprint ed., Gloucester, MA: Peter Smith, 1965.

Van Camp, Leonard. "Choral Balance and the Alto Part in Early American Choral Music." Choral Journal 15 (May 1975): 7-9.

Wienandt, Elwyn A., and Robert H. Young. The Anthem in England and America. New York: Free Press, 1970.

__________, eds. Fifteen Anthems from America. Glen Rock, NJ: J. Fischer, 1970.

Wunderlich, Charles E. "A History and Bibliography of Early American Periodicals, 1782–1852." Ph.D. dissertation, University of Michigan, 1962.

CHRONOLOGICAL SUMMARY OF ANTE-BELLUM FOUR-SHAPE TUNEBOOKS

Year	*Compiler(s), Short Title*	*Other Editions*	*Rural*	*Urban*	*Related Information*
1798?	Little, Smith, *Easy Instructor*	[1801], [1802], 1803, 1805, 1806, 1807, 1807, 1808, [1809], [1810], [1810], [1811], [1812], [1813], [1813], [1813], [1814], [1814], [1815], [1815], [1816], [1816], [1817], [1817], [1818], 1818, [1819], 1819, [1820], 1820, [1822], [1824], [1826], 1828, [1830], 1831	X	X	
1803	Law, *Art of Singing*	Later partial editions		X	Round notes earlier: later seven-shape
1803	Smith, W., *Easy Instructor II*	[1806]	X		
1807	Husband, *Collection*		X	X	
1807	Husband, *Philadelphia Harmony*	1811		X	
1807	Law, *Harmonic Companion*	[after 1807]		X	Some seven-shape
1807	Woodward and Aitken, *Ecclesiae*	[ca. 1807], 1809	X	X	
1809	Fobes, *Delaware Harmony*	1814		X	
1809	Gillet, *Maryland Selection*		X	X	
[1809]	Law, *Art of Playing*			X	
[ca. 1810]	[*Collection*]		X	X	Some round notes
1810	Doll, *Leichte unterricht*	1814, 1821	X	X	
1810	Wyeth, *Repository* [I]	1811, 1812, 1818, 1820, 1826, 1834	X	X	

CHRONOLOGICAL SUMMARY OF ANTE-BELLUM FOUR-SHAPE TUNEBOOKS

Year	*Compiler (s), Short Title*	*Other Editions*	*Rural*	*Urban*	*Related Information*
[1811]	Law, *Select Harmony*				
1812	Woodward, *Sacred . . . Miniature*			X	
1813	Patterson, *Church Music*	1815	X		
1813	Wyeth, *Repository II*	1820	X	X	
1814	Lewis, *Beauties*	1816, 1818, 1820, 1828, 1831, 1835	X	X	
1815	Doll, *Leichter unterricht II*		X	X	
1815	M'Cormick, *Western Harmonist*		X		
1816	Armstrong, *Pittsburgh Selection*			X	
1816	Davisson, *Kentucky Harmony*	1817, 1819, 1821, 1826	X	X (later editions)	
1816	Flint, *Columbian Harmonist*			X	
1816	Funk, *Nützliche Choral*		X	X	
1817	Gillet, *Virginia Sacred*		X	X	
1817	Nevius, Van Deventer, and Frazee, *New Brunswick Collection*	1818, 1822, 1827, 1829, 1832, 1835, 1838, 1840, 1841	X	X	
1818	Boyd, *Virginia Sacred*		X	X	
1818	Gerhart and Eyer, *Choral-Harmonie*	1822	X	X	
1818	Johnson, *Tennessee Harmony*	1821	X		
1818	Metcalfe, *Kentucky Harmonist*	1820, 1826	X		
1820	Caldwell, *Union Harmony*	1837	X	X	

CHRONOLOGICAL SUMMARY OF ANTE-BELLUM FOUR-SHAPE TUNEBOOKS

Year	*Compiler (s), Short Title*	*Other Editions*	*Rural*	*Urban*	*Related Information*
1820	Carden, *Missouri Harmony*	1825, 1827, 1830, 1831, 1832, 1833, 1834, 1835, 1836, 1837, 1838, 1839, 1840, 1841, 1842, 1844, 1846, 1848, 1850, 1855, 1857	X	X (supplement)	Also round notes ca. 1848
1820	Carrell, *Songs of Zion*				Unlocated
1820	Davisson, *Supplement*	[ca. 1823], 1826	X		
1821	Davisson, *Introduction*		X		Duplicates 1816
1821	Rothbaust, *Franklin Harmonie*	[1830]	X	X	
1822	Ely, *Sacred Music*			X	
1822	St. John, *American Harmonist*			X	
1824	Carden, Rogers, Moore, and Green, *Western Harmonist*		X	X	
1824	Lewis, *Songs of Zion*		X	X	
1825	Davisson, *Small Collection*	[ca. 1826]	X		Contents from 1821
1825	Knight, *Juvenile Harmony*	1829, 1831, 1833, 1836	X		
1825	Moore, *Columbian Harmony*		X		
1827	Bentz, *Neue Harmonie*		X		
1827	Hutson, *Pennsylvania Harmonist*			X	
1829	Carden, *United States Harmony*		X	X	

CHRONOLOGICAL SUMMARY OF ANTE-BELLUM FOUR-SHAPE TUNEBOOKS

Year	*Compiler (s), Short Title*	*Other Editions*	*Rural*	*Urban*	*Related Information*
1829	Cole, *Union Harmony*			X	
1831	Clayton and Carrell, *Virginia Harmony*	1836		X	
1831	Rhinehart, *American or Union*		X	X	
1831	Smith, H., *Church Harmony*	1834, 1837, 1841, 1847		X	
1831	Snyder and Chappell, *Western Lyre*	1835	X	X	
[after 1831]	Schmidt, *Supplement*				
1832	Funk, *Genuine Church Music*	1835, 1842, 1847	X	X	Round notes later
1832	Gordon and Haynes, *Sweets*		X		
1832	Hickok, *Sacred Harp*	Included in 1834	X	X	
1832	Palmer, *Western Harmonic*	1833	X	X	Round notes earlier
1832	Wakefield, *Christian's Harp*	1837	X		
1832	Willis, *Lexington Cabinet*		X		
1833	Eyer, *Union Choral Harmony*	1836, 1839	X	X	
1833	*Methodist Harmonist*			X	*Harmonist,* 1837, continues
1834	Hickok and Fleming, *Evangelical Musick and Sacred Harp*	1834, 1836, 1837, 1839, 1839, 1840, 1840, 1841, 1847, 1847, [1848]	X	X	Includes 1832
1834	Mason, L., and T. Mason, *Sacred Harp*	1835, 1836, 1836, 1840, 1841, 1847		X	Also round notes 1837
1834	Mason, T., [and L. Mason], *Ohio Sacred Harp*				Unlocated
1835	Hayden, *Introduction*	1838	X	X	

CHRONOLOGICAL SUMMARY OF ANTE-BELLUM FOUR-SHAPE TUNEBOOKS

Year	*Compiler (s), Short Title*	*Other Editions*	*Rural*	*Urban*	*Related Information*
1835	Walker, *Southern Harmony*	[1835], 1845, 1847, 1847, 1851, 1854, 1854	X		1846
1836	Steffey, *Valley Harmonist*	1845	X		
1836	*Zion's Harp*				Unlocated
1837	Caldwell, *Union Harmony*		X	X	
1837	*Harmonist*	1840, 1841, 1842, 1843, 1844, 1845		X	*Methodist Harmonist,* 1833
1838	Jackson, J. B., *Knoxville Harmony*	1840	X		
1840	Hickok, *Social Lyrist*	1843, 1847	X	X	
1840	*Pennsylvänische Sammlung*	1844	X	X	
[1842]	[Hastings], *Sacred Songs*	[1842], 1842, 1855		X	Round notes earlier
1844	Musselmann, *Die neue choral*	1853	X	X	
1844	Wakefield, *Western Harp*	1846		X	
1844	Weber, *Pennsylvania Choral*	1859, 1867, 1870	X	X	
1844	White and King, *Sacred Harp*	1847, 1850, 1859, 1860, 1869, 1902, 1909, 1911, 1911, 1929, 1936, 1949, 1960, 1960, 1966, 1971	X		
1845	Hunter and Wakefield, *Minstrel of Zion*	1850, 1854	X	X	
1846	Hood, *Southern Church*			X	
1846	Walker, *Southern and Western*		X		Appendix to 1835
[1848]	Hauser, *Hesperian Harp*	1852	X	X	

CHRONOLOGICAL SUMMARY OF ANTE-BELLUM FOUR-SHAPE TUNEBOOKS

Year	*Compiler (s), Short Title*	*Other Editions*	*Rural*	*Urban*	*Related Information*
1848	Hendrickson, *Union Harmony*		X		Later seven-shape
1848	Jackson, S., and Goodbon, *Sacred Harmony*			X	Also round notes
1848	Rhinehart, *American Church*	1850, 1856	X	X	
1849	Ball, *Manual*		X		
1849	Dingley, *Devotional Harmonist*	1853		X	Also round notes
1849	Jones, *Southern Minstrel*		X	X	
1852	Weber, *Juvenile Harmony*	1859	X	X	
1853	Weber, *Neue Choral*	1855			Unlocated
1853	Woodbury, *Harp*			X	Also round notes
1854	Winebrenner and Meignen, *Seraphina*			X	Also round notes
1855	McCurry, *Social Harp*	1859, 1868	X		
1855	Weber, *Juvenile Singing*				Unlocated
1855	Weber, *New Harmony*				Unlocated
1859	Weber, *Pennsylvänische Sammlung*		X	X	

TITLE INDEX TO AUTHORS

Harp of the South—Woodbury
Hesperian Harp—Hauser

Introduction to Sacred Music—Hayden
Introduction to Sacred Music . . . from the Kentucky Harmony—Davisson

Johnson's Tennessee Harmony—Johnson
Juvenile Harmony—Knight
Juvenile Harmony—Weber
Juvenile Singing School—Weber

Kentucky Harmonist—Metcalfe
Kentucky Harmony—Davisson
Knoxville Harmony—Jackson, John

Leichter Unterricht—Doll
Lexington Cabinet—Willis

Manual of the Sacred Choir—Ball
Maryland Selection—Gillet
Methodist Harmonist—(see title)
Minstrel of Zion—Hunter
Missouri Harmony—Carden
Musical Magazine—Law
Musical Primer—Law

Neue choral Harmonie—Musselmann
Neue Choral Harmonie—Weber
Neue Harmonie—Bentz
Neue Harmonie—Weber
New-Brunswick Collection—Nevius *et al.*
New Harmony—Weber

Ohio Sacred Harp—Mason, T.
Original Sacred Harp—(see title)

Patterson's Church Music—Patterson
Pennsylvänische Choral Harmonie—Weber

Pennsylvänische Sammlung—(see title)
Pennsylvänische Sammlung—Weber
Pennsylvania Harmonist—Hutson
Philadelphia Harmony—Adgate
Pittsburgh Selection—Armstrong

Repository of Sacred Music—Willis
Repository of Sacred Music—Wyeth

Sacred Harmony—Jackson, S., and Goodbon
Sacred Harp—Hickok; Hickok and Fleming
Sacred Harp—Mason and Mason
Sacred Harp—White and King; White and White
Sacred Minstrel—Hickok and Fleming
Sacred Music—Ely
Sacred Music in Miniature—Woodward
Sacred Songs for Family and Social—Hastings
Sammlung von Kirchen-Musik—Bentz
Select Harmony—Law
Selection of Sacred Music—Woodward and Aitken
Seraphina—Winebrenner and Meignen
Small Collection . . . from the Kentucky Harmony—Davisson
Social Harp—McCurry
Social Lyrist—Hickok
Songs of Zion—Carrell
Songs of Zion—Lewis
Southern and Western Pocket Harmonist—Walker
Southern Church Melodist—Hood
Southern Harmony—Walker
Southern Minstrel—Jones
Supplement to the Church Harmony—[Smith] Schmidt, H.
Supplement to the Kentucky Harmony—Davisson
Sweets of Music—Gordon and Haynes

Tennessee Harmony—Johnson

Union Choral Harmonie—Eyer
Union Harmonist—Rhinehart
Union Harmony—Caldwell
Union Harmony—Cole
Union Harmony—Hendrickson
United States Harmony—Carden

Valley Harmonist—Steffey
Virginia Harmony—Clayton and Carrell
Virginia Sacred Minstrel—Gillet
Virginia Sacred Music Repository—Boyd

Western Harmonic Companion—Palmer
Western Harmonist—M'Cormick
Western Harmony—Carden *et al.*
Western Harp—Wakefield
Western Lyre—Snyder and Chappell
Wyeth's Repository of Sacred Music—Wyeth

Zion's Harp—(see title)

ADDENDA

Publishers often send books in the page-proof stage to reviewers, hoping for early reviews but knowing full well, if despairingly, that they will have no chance to reflect the reviewers' critiques in the published volume. With this monograph the publisher has been more fortunate. Proofs of the camera-ready copy, about to go to the printer, were read critically by revival-hymnody specialist Paul C. Echols, with such diligence and dispatch that we were able to amend details of Professor Stanislaw's text and to offer the following addenda, which could not be entered in the monograph proper. We are grateful to Mr. Echols for his careful critique and to Professor Stanislaw for his approval of the amendments.

NB: The "-a" entries among the Addenda, which are tunebooks or editions added to the basic checklist, are not reflected in the material on pages 49-58.

H. Wiley Hitchcock, Director, I. S. A. M.

5 [Added information] 152, 16 pp.

Bilingual collection with title, rudiments, and hymn texts appearing in English and German. The last 16 pp. are an appendix of German chorale tunes to German texts.

62a Fast, J. J. **Die Cantica Sacra**; eine Sammlung von Kirchengesängen, enthaltend, enbst einigen neuen stücken, eine Auserlesene Auswahl deutscher und englischer Choraele, Choralgesaenge, Psalmodie, etc. entnommen den besten Werken Europa's und Amerika's . . . mit deutschem und Englischem Texte. Hudson, OH: Hudson Book Co., c.1854.

18 cm. 352 pp.
CTY DLC ICN MOSCS PPLT

82a 1887. New York: T. Mason and G. Lane.
IAU

97 [Delete entry (same as 98).]

131a Leavitt, Joshua (1794-1873). **The Christian Lyre**: Adapted for Use in Families, Prayer Meetings, and Revivals of Religion. The Music printed in Patent Notes. First Patent Note Edition. New York: Published by Jonathan Leavitt, 1832 (c.1830).

14 cm. 216 pp.
MB MWA NBUG NNUT NRCR PPPRHI RPB

131b Leonard, Silas W. (1814-1870) and A. D. Fillmore. **The Christian Psalmist**, A Collection of Tunes and Hymns of various Metres, original and selected: For the use of The Church of God, Bible Classes, and Singing Societies, Embracing the Round Note, the Numeral, and the Patent Note Systems of Notation. Cincinnati: n.p. Stereotyped by E. Shepard, 1847.

5.3 x 4 inches. 383 pp.
MWA

195 [Delete entry (round-note).]

196 [Delete entry (round-note).]

197 [Delete entry (round-note).]

198 [Delete entry (round-note).]

199 [Delete entry (round-note).]

200 [Delete entry (round-note).]

233a 3rd ed. improved and enlarged. **The Church Harmony**. Containing a Selection of Approved Psalm and Hymn Tunes . . . Including also a Second Part of Supplement, Containing a Variety of Tunes suitable for Singing Schools and Private Societies. Chambersburg, PA: Printed for the proprietor by Henry Ruby. 1834.

152, 79, [1] pp.
MWA

242a 1835. Cincinnati: Published by W. L. Chappell and Corey & Fairbank. (The extra 40 pp. comprise a "Supplement to the Western Lyre. Consisting Principally of Anthems and Set Pieces. By W. L. Chappell")

184, 40 pp.
MWA

242b 2nd ed. Cincinnati: Published by W. L. Chappell, c.1841 (no date on t.p.).

184 pp.
CTY DLC MWA NNUT RPB

244a Wakefield, Samuel (1799-1895). **The American Repository of Sacred Music,** containing a great variety of psalm and hymn tunes, original and selected . . . Pittsburgh: Printed and published by Cramer & Spear, 1830.

188, 21-30, [2] p. (after p. 188 the pagination begins again, confusingly, at p. 21)
RPB

246 [Added information] Cincinnati: Published by Johnston & Stockton. 164, 64 pp.

249 **The Western Harp:** Containing a Collection of Sacred Music, Original and Selected . . . Together with a Concise Introduction to the Art of Singing. Third edition. With valuable and large additions. Pittsburgh: Charles H. Kay, 1846.

224 pp.
MWA

251a 1838. Stereotype edition, corrected and improved. Spartanburg, SC: Published by the Author.

32, 218 pp.
MWA

261a 1859. 2d ed. **The Juvenile Harmony,** Containing A Choice Collection of Moral and Sacred Songs, Designed for Juvenile Singing Schools, Common Schools, Sunday Schools, Family Circles and Juvenile Concerts. Printed by the Compiler.

267a 1854. 4th ed. Published by the compiler.

16, 376 pp.
CTHC DC

269a 1869. 7th ed. Allentown, PA: E. D. Leisenring & Co. (c.1859)

16, 352, 6 pp.
MWA

288a 1836. Latest improved edition. Cincinnati: J. A. James & Co.

200 pp.
NN

Richard J. Stanislaw, Professor of Music at Bloomsburg State College, has the degrees of Doctor of Musical Arts in choral music from the University of Illinois, Master of Music and Bachelor of Music Education from Temple University, and Bachelor of Science in sacred music from Philadelphia College of Bible. Among his awards have been a research grant from the National Endowment for the Humanities and a creative teaching award at Bloomsburg.

The Institute for Studies in American Music at Brooklyn College, established in 1971, is a division of the Department of Music in the college's School of the Performing Arts. The Institute contributes to the field of American-music studies by publishing a monograph series, bibliographies, and a newsletter. It encourages and supports research by sponsoring fellowships for distinguished scholars and is currently supervising the series *Recent Researches in American Music,* published by A-R Editions, Inc. I.S.A.M. activities also include concerts held at Brooklyn College for students, faculty, and the public. In addition to serving as an information center, the Institute participates in conferences and symposia dealing with all areas of American music, including art music, popular music, and the music of oral tradition. In 1974, I.S.A.M. co-sponsored (with Yale University) the Charles Ives Centennial Festival-Conference and, in 1977, The Phonograph and Our Musical Life, a conference exploring the humanistic impact on our musical culture of the phonograph and sound-recording in general.